MY BRING UP

SHIRLY HOOK

Illustrated by
AMY HOOK-THERRIEN

Korongo Books

My Bring Up, by Shirly Hook

ISBN: 978-1-943741-12-0

Direct inquiries to sara@korongobooks.com.

Contents

Introduction

A number of years ago, my youngest daughter asked what we did for fun when we were younger. I told her a few stories, and she replied, "But Mom, we don't have those type of memories." I told her that it was the era, the 1950s and '60s. A lot of families were really poor, and they had to have an imagination to go along with it. I was taken back, because both of my daughters have done a lot more than I had ever done at their ages. They have traveled all over the world and have done many adventures.

So my stories begin.

Imagination of
West Hill Kids

Imagination of West Hill Kids

There were four of us kids, rather close in age. My mother would put us outside to play very early in the morning, and we didn't go back inside until we had to get cleaned up before Dad came home. We were more or less on our own. A bathroom was no problem, because we didn't have one. It was the old outhouse, with the Sears and Roebuck catalog. That was all we needed.

About noon, we would go to the door, and she would hand out peanutbutter sandwiches to all of us. To quench our thirst, we had a water house, where we just opened our mouth under the spigot and got our fill.

If it was too cold in the morning, we would go lay down on top of the old Holstein cow. Her name was Moochie Cow. It must have been a sight for anyone to drive by and see four kids draped all over the forgiving cow. She would just chew her cud and patiently wait until the last kid slid off her back. She would slowly get up and walk to the brook for her long-awaited drink.

My aunt Dot and uncle Mel gave my sister and me matching cowgirl outfits that their girls grew out of. We would pretend we were in the Wild West with our six-shooters at our side and our steed ready for the action. There was no problem that we didn't have a fancy horse. We had super cows. We would climb up on the barbed-wire fence and lasso the cows and climb on. This worked well with ol' Moochie. She would amble around the pasture, going down the cow paths, gently taking care of her cargo.

One day, I had a brainstorm. Why not get on the Jersey heifer? She seemed lively and ran like the wind. Believe me, she did. I got her close to the fence and popped on like a bullet, and we were off. She tried to buck me off and then, like a streak, headed for the lower pasture. My brothers and sister were so excited. They were cheering me on. They never saw such a show, and it was live. I hung on for dear life, but I didn't make the eight seconds. She finally bucked a last time, and I went flying into the air and landed in a heap with the wind knocked out of me. That was the last time I rode that bugger.

In the winter, we used to go sliding. My gram would give us the inserts to the old steamer trunks for sleds. We would put the old wire-rim sunglasses on with one of Gram's fancy straw hats, and away we would go. Glare ice was the best!

My dad used to deal in junk cars. Bits and pieces to all sorts of automobiles were everywhere. The four of us decided that we needed a new way to slide. At that point, we didn't have a sled, not even the inserts to the trunks. The only idea we had at that point was check out the junkyard. Just perhaps there would be an answer there.

We were in luck. Laying before our eyes was a

gleaming car hood, shining brightly at us like a brand-new car. God knows, Dad had a million of them. He probably wouldn't miss one. We went to the old barn and fetched some bailer twine, tied it to the hood, and with the help of our old dog dragged it up to the ledges.

You could not have asked for better conditions. *Glare ice.* I could almost feel how the professional skiers feel with such conditions, warm and fuzzy. We all hopped into the hood, including our dog. With the hood teetering on the edge of the ledge, away we went, hella hooping. The screams were almost terror-like, hitting rocks, trees, and whatever else was in our path. We would lose some of the passengers, but that was okay, because we couldn't stop. We sometimes would sail right through the barbed-wire fences with only a few minor scratches. The hood would finally come to rest at the bottom of the hill. Breathless, shaking, terror-struck, but you wouldn't admit it. We would hitch the dog up and trudge up the hill once more, and make another run of it. I imagine we looked like a Calvin and Hobbs comic strip. I must grin to myself.

When we were finished with the hood, we put it back in its place. It was rather scratched and dented, really in pretty bad shape.

Dad did find it a few weeks later and asked what happened to it. We thought the aliens probably came down from outer space and had powers to bend and twist it into its present state. Dad just looked at us and shook his head.

Our mother would always make us take our younger brother with us. He was about two years old, and he crimped our style, if you know what I mean. We were told to let him do the same stuff we were doing. We looked at each other with crossed eyes and said, "All-righty then."

At this point, we had acquired two used sleds with runners. We had a contest of sorts, who could go down the hill and under the barbed-wire fence without ripping our clothes off. It was doable. We had done it many times before. But this time it was different. We had a pest of a brother that we had to bring along. There he was, standing there in his little brown snowsuit, with pull-on rubber boots and an Elmer Fudd hat that wasn't fastened. I clambered onto the sled; my sister put him on the back and told him to hold on. For a two-year-old, we thought he should know what to do.

Well, the conditions were an A-plus. Glare ice. My sister and other brother gave me a super deluxe shove down the hill, and away we went. Except Bruce forgot to hang on. He managed to get his foot caught in the runner, he fell off, and I dragged him clear to China. There was no way to stop the sled, because it had a mind of its own. We finally came to a screaming halt. Mother thought I killed him, but it was only a few minor scratches on his dear little face. For me, I got yelled at. It was a long while before dear little brother was allowed to go sliding with us.

Dad always had a good supply of old tires, any size you could ever dream of. So, what are we going to do with them? That was a good question. There must be something that our creative minds could come up with.

Low and behold, didn't we come up with a super idea. Why not roll them up the hill and then get inside of them and see how far you could go? Bingo, another grand idea.

It was a long hill up, but coming down was

another story. With sweat dripping off our brow, we finally made it to the top. Sitting for a minute before we went whirling down the steep grade, we discussed which direction each of us would take. After long thoughts, we steadied our rides and climbed aboard and pushed off. We didn't factor in the dizzy part, and that was what happened. All I could see was rocks, trees . . . "Oh, Lord, there goes the wire fence, and Dad is going to kill us," and then the stone wall, up and over, and right into the road.

I staggered out and put a victory smile on, even though it didn't feel that way. We just had to figure out a way to mend the fence before Dad got home, or just say the cows got into some bees that stung them and they went through the fence, saw them do it, with fingers crossed behind our back.

———

My Bring Up

My Bring Up

I was brought up in the hills of Chelsea. Actually, it was West Hill. I had my parents, my sister, and two younger brothers. We lived in somewhat of a shack of sorts, but at that age it was home. My parents called it the trailer house because it had a couple of wheels attached to it. I called it the tin house or the old shack.

It consisted of a bedroom at the end, where my parents slept. It was big enough for a bed and little else. Then there was the living area, consisting of a blue velvet couch that was given to my parents at some point. There was a path between that and the bunk beds, where us girls slept. Then the kitchen area, which had a wood stove for winter heat and winter cooking. There was a window behind it, and the stovepipe went through one of the panes. Next there was an electric stove that looked like the one on the Lucille Ball show. Perhaps Dad found it at the junkyard and repaired it. At the very end of the structure was a sink. The water pipe came through the wall and ran the most cool, delicious water ever. The water came from the well house, which came from the woods up the hill. At one time there was a small table by the sink. However, that changed when my brother was born. A crib was placed there, which was made by our grandfather. A small window was above the crib. I remember the window, due to the fact the one goldfish would freeze once in awhile. We would move his container and unthaw him, and he always survived. There was no bathroom; we had an outhouse up the path. During the summer months it wasn't too bad, but in the winter, you didn't want to linger too long looking at the Sears and Roebuck catalog and making a wish list. No, sirree. For bathing, we would heat the water on the stove and wash as best as we could. When we were little we were put in the sink.

There wasn't much room in there. We lived in that little space for a long time. When the youngest was born, this all changed. We needed more room. My grandfather and Dad put an addition on. The room was big enough for all us kids. It was just rough-cut lumber. It was quite fun, because the two-by-fours were like a shelf to put little treasures on. Tarpaper was put on the outside so the wind wouldn't howl too bad through the little cracks.

We did share our space with a small creature: a pigeon, named Buzzer Bird. He was a homing pigeon that was blown off course during a storm. He was in pretty poor health. Of course, my mother brought him in so he would be warm. He stayed in a little cage-type thing unless we decided that he needed to stretch his wings and he was let out. Mom didn't agree with us, and she would get upset. We would finally catch the ol' buzzer and put him back into his space. We also had an Airedale dog named Brownie that took up residence in our room.

We did have Christmas, but I don't recall any tree. I remember that we did hang our stockings up the night before, and they would have an orange, perhaps a few nuts. One year, my father said to us girls which hand we wanted. Behind his back he had two dolls dressed in pj's. One had blue pj's on, and the other had red. I picked the red one.

One year, my brother had appendicitis, and money was nearly nonexisting. He was about two years old, and he was in the Barre hospital for a real long time. They would only let him look out the window and wave while we waited in the car. Some people from the West Hill church arrived one morning. They asked me what I wanted for Christmas. I replied, "I want my brother to come home." They were very kind to us. They had some gifts for Christmas morning.

When I was about nine or ten, our grandmother passed over. At that point, we moved into her house.

The old tin house sat vacant for many decades, until it was pulled down and put to sleep for the very last time.

———

The Fall of
the Year

The Fall of the Year

The final days of summer approached, and it was time for the children to go to school. Most of the harvesting was finished, just a few more chores to do before settling in for the long winter. Wood gathering was usually done on cooler days of fall. It had seasoned perhaps a year or so, to make sure it was dry, then it was put into a woodshed or in the cellar.

The canned vegetables were labeled and carried down to the cool cellar, where cabbages were hanging from twine from the ceiling. Potatoes, probably twenty to thirty bushels, were in the darkness of their room, in the bins. Later on, toward the first snow, the hogs would be butchered and smoked in a drum that was made for that purpose. They too would be strung up and hung from the rafters. Perhaps a steer, if we were lucky enough to have one, would be processed in jars and enjoyed throughout the winter. Venison would be taken during hunting season and canned.

The schools usually started after Labor Day, due to the harvesting.

I remember my Grandmother Hook was big

on education. She would work with my sister and me, endlessly teaching reading, writing, and arithmetic. She made sure we knew this at a very young age.

My sister was going to first grade, and she was so excited. I tried to be excited for her, but deep down, I couldn't, or didn't want to. My parents and Gram were getting everything she needed: a new lunch box, shoes, perhaps a new outfit, and don't forget socks and new undergarments. We were in the garden, and Gram and Guy delivered the goods the day before the big day. I was sitting as the scene unfolded. Patty was all dolled up, mother was taking photos, and I was pouting. My Gram tried to explain everything to me, that I would be going to school next year. I did not want to hear it. I wanted to go now.

Gram sat down beside me and handed me a little brown sack. Inside was a little doll in a berry basket. I still, pouting, wanted a lunch box. After a fashion, Gram got up and wandered off. I followed her, leaving the little doll, with blinking eyes, in among the roses.

Gram said, "Aren't you going to bring your baby along? She will be lonely there, all by herself."

I looked at her and replied, "I guess I had better. The bears will eat her."

I still have that little baby doll. She is in the glass cabinet, where she blinks her eyes at you if you look just right.

———

Aunt Bea and Uncle Fred

Aunt Bea and Uncle Fred

Going back to the 1950s and 1960s, I can remember my great-aunt Bea and uncle Fred. We would go to their apartment for the Thanksgiving gathering. The apartment would be overflowing with my mother's side of the family. I have no idea how they squeezed them all into that tiny little place. We would have the most delicious meal. The turkey was rubbed down by lard, seasoned, tied, and put in a brown paper bag that was also covered with lard, then thrown into the oven to fill the room with the most beautiful aroma. Homemade gravies, squash, mashed potatoes, succotash, rolls, and homemade apple pie with sage cheese. It was wonderful.

Aunt Bea was of very short stature. She had short gray hair, gold-rimmed glasses, and a twinkle in her eye. Uncle Fred was rather tall with snow-white hair, gold-rimmed glasses, and a pipe between his lips. He sat in his glider rocker and rocked and told stories.

Uncle Fred said they had married in 1904. They lived in Randolph, where he farmed and worked at the Bethel quarry. They moved to Saint

Albans, where he worked for the Central Vermont Railroad as a fireman. They journeyed to California and he worked for the railroad again. He told stories of them sleeping under the stars in their bedrolls. Aunt Bea would have her trusty little derringer under her pillow. They later moved to West Hill, where they had their farm, and they operated a sawmill in the village. In 1944 they moved to Chelsea, where he was employed by the funeral home. This is where I remembered them.

They lived in the middle of nowhere, the most beautiful land you could only dream of. There was a babbling brook, a little white house, and a barn of sorts. I never visited them there, because I wasn't born yet. However, when I was a bit older, perhaps nine or ten, I would walk from my parents' place over to the old farmstead. Sitting there in the sun, listening to the singing brook, I would daydream about living there. Going into the abandoned house, exploring, sometimes finding an old forgotten photo or some other treasures would fill the soul.

They moved to the village, into an apartment over the funeral home. There they lived until they passed. My sister and I would go and help them with little chores. One day Aunt Bea wanted me to give her insulin shots, for she was a diabetic. I told her I couldn't because I would hurt her. She just chuckled and gave her own self the insulin.

I always wondered why they never had children, for they were great with children. Her sister didn't have children either. I never gave it a thought after they had passed, but a few years later, Mother started to write about her family and her childhood. She started her story with how they lived and survived during the hard times. This is where I was saddened to read about why they never had children.

She told that her aunts and some of my father's aunts and cousins were sterilized by the doctors. I remember my father's aunts, and they never had children either. They also lived in Chelsea. It seemed odd that so many of the families, on both sides, never had children.

It seemed that a man by the name of Professor Henry Perkins, of UVM, led the eugenics program starting in the early 1920s. He was a fan of Hitler and his ideas of a perfect society in Germany. He, with others, pressured the state to pass a bill.

A bill was passed in 1931, *An Act for Human Betterment by Voluntary Sterilization*. Vermont was the twenty-fifth state to have such a bill.

Strange enough, Governor Stanley Wilson, who resided in Chelsea, signed the bill.

The state would find and isolate village and farm families that had bad genetic traits—in other words, nonwhite Vermonters. At times, children were taken from them; crosses would be burned. I remember that happening. They called them gypsies, pirates, and river rats. It was pure hell for these people. I remember them being called gypsies. This is when the Abenaki people told no one who they were and where they came from.

I believe that sterilization started a long time before it was passed by the state, and continued longer than it was reported. I recall stories of sterilization being done into the 1960s and 1970s.

About twenty years ago, I called a family relative and asked her about the sterilization. She stated, "What's in the closet, stays in the closet," and she hung up, never to be heard from again.

I asked my mother how some of the people avoided sterilization. She replied, "Because they went to the logging camps, and stayed."

———

A Man Named
Guy Rand

A Man Named
Guy Rand

My Grandfather Hook passed over when my dad was still in high school. My gram remarried at some point, a man named Guy Rand. He was a gentle soul, quick to laugh, a downright good person. He owned a junkyard in Randolph Center on Rand Road. He was also a peddler. He peddled his wares from town to town, house to house. If Guy didn't have it, you didn't need it.

I always thought it would be great to become a peddler, and I thought it might be my vocation in the future. I imagined the adventures I would have and the people I would meet and the places I would see. What a life that would be! I guess that was through the eyes of a kid, but now I am thinking perhaps that kid was right. Damn straight. I still have time to be a peddler!

Guy would load up his old blue GMC with dishes, bread, candy, oversized Vermont crackers —you name it and he had it. He used to arrive at the parents' house, and us kids would look over his gold mine and wonder what he had lurking in the tiny corners. One day, I spied a little cake pan that I really thought was cute, for twenty-five cents. Twenty-five cents more than I had. Guy wanted to give it to me, but I said no. I saved all summer to buy that darling little tin. When I got it, I placed it in a safe place. I still have it, and when I see it, I think of Guy.

I loved to go to Guy's place. A lot of times, us kids would get up early and ride over on the doodlebug. It usually was cold, but you didn't mind, you were going to Gram's and Guy's. It was such a fun place to go. The old house sat across from the junkyard. Giant hollyhocks grew around the front, in every color of the rainbow. As you walked into the front room, a giant table was placed in the middle, loaded down with all sorts of things. We would walk around the table, curious as a cat, not to touch, but touch with your eyes. Fascinating things, flashlights, socks, parts, candy, marshmallow cookies, pots, pans, the list went on. In the back room was a real delight, Vermont Common Crackers, by the case. These weren't like the little doll-sized ones we have today, no sirree, these were hungry-man crackers. A couple of those puppies would fill a bowl; you break them up and pour cold milk over the top. What a treat! No matter where you looked, there were crackers. It looked like cracker heaven to me.

Guy had an old Airedale that was brother to one we had. He was very intelligent and funny. When us kids would walk into the old house, Brownie would be going to each of us, wagging his overweight body in time with the music playing on the radio. He wasn't just checking us out, he was looking for an opportunity to grab something of ours and run as fast as his fat body could go. In the winter, it was our mittens, if they weren't safety-pinned on or connected with a string. He would take the chance and grab them and take off like a bullet. Gram would be tight behind him, her handmade housedress blowing in the breeze and the grandmother shoes tapping loudly against the floor. He would motor around the old table as fast as he could go. It was like a race track. Finally, Gram and the old dog had to stop, because they were running out of breath. Gulping for air, they both finally sit down. We would eye the dog to see if he was going to take off, but he was just waiting, mittens soggy with drool hanging out of his mouth. He would eyeball Gram, and she would eye him back, knowing what was on his mind: a glorious treat. Gram would finally give in. Heading for the table, she would pick up a package of marshmallow cookies and hand one to the dog. He would surrender the mittens, and he would look like the cat that ate the canary.

The old dog had another trick he would pull. If someone came to the house to buy something, they would usually lay the money down on the corner of the table. The little robber would eyeball the money, zip around, grab it, and run like blue blazes. He had their number and which button to push. We always got a chuckle out of him. He was very entertaining.

Guy had many surprises for us. One day we went to visit him, and Guy said, "Got something for you young'uns." We followed him like a parade of ducks. He had a large cardboard box, and a whistling noise was coming from inside. What could he have for us? He slowly opened the flaps, and out popped two guinea pigs. They looked like a dust mop with eyes. They whistled and made funny noises, weird little creatures. Guy said, "Got these for ya, and you gotta take them home." Oh, yeah, that was going to be easy, not.

Guy took the hairy little guys over to the car to put them in the back seat, and Dad was standing there. Guy said to Dad, "Got these for the young'uns, and they gotta take them home."

Dad replied, "No, they can't have them. We have enough animals."

It was like a ping-pong match for a while. Guy would get a couple of points, and then Dad would. Finally, Dad said, "When I say no, it means no, understand?" Guy turned a little and smiled, and winked and said no more.

We ventured to the junkyard and was wondering how we would get the little pigs home. No fear. Guy had it covered. Just before we were headed home, Guy placed the little animals in the back of the car. They scrambled under the seat without a word. We pretended we didn't know what just happened. We were innocent, had no part in this. It went well the first part of the journey, but out of the blue, there was a sharp whistle. The little mops were going to get us in trouble! We pretended that we didn't hear anything, but Dad did.

"What is that noise? Knock it off. You kids, stop it."

Lucky for us, the pigs quieted down, and arrived home. We jumped out of the car as fast as we could and waited for Dad to go and get the milk pail for milking. We knew if we could show them to Mother, that she wouldn't say no. She loved animals, more than humans. We finally got the little buggers from under the seat by putting some apples down. We held them like babies and took them into the house. We hit the nail on the head: She thought they were darling. We scored, and she said we could keep them. Dad was upset. But as we pointed out, Guy did it. We knew nothing about it.

My Gram would let us jump on Guy's bed. I have no idea why. We couldn't jump on hers. We would have a blast, flying high in the air and hitting the ceiling. We would jump so much we could hardly catch our breath. Finally, the mattress would fall off, and Gram would put it back on, and away we would go again until Dad showed up and put an end to our fun.

My Gram passed on, and Guy was lost. One winter morning, he got in touch with Dad and told him there was something wrong with his old dog. Dad drove over to see him. Guy had loaded this best friend on the sled. The dog looked really sick, hardly alive. Guy had tears streaming down his old weathered face. The old Airedale was old and tired. He had a good life, and Gram kinda overdid the cookies, but that was the way it was. Dad put him to rest and we tried to comfort Guy.

Guy loved the Red Socks and never missed the game on WDEV. The radio was his companion after my gram passed. The telephone rang; it was Guy. The radio was on the blink. He went over and fixed it. Guy was happy. At this point of his life, he was nearly blind.

The last time I remember Guy was when he said he had something for us girls. He handed my grandmother's wedding band, from 1912, and a gold watch to me. The watch was still in its original box. My grandfather had bought it for her for sixty dollars. This was close to 1912. There was a ruby ring and a diamond ring. My sister was gifted them. He was in poor health and close to totally blind. I hope he knew how important he was to me. I will always remember him, his kindness and the love he showed to us.

Guy was something else. He is truly missed.

———

Milking Old
Moochie

6

Milking Old Moochie

One day we were heading down the cow path to the brook, looking for something to do. We heard a little cry of sorts. We investigated, and what to our wonder but a batch of kittens. They were no bigger than nothing. Their little eyes were not open. They cried for their mama, but to no avail. We trotted home to get the baby buggy. Someone had given us a flashy old buggy that really worked. The wheels worked, even the little hood went up and down as it should. We were in heaven when we acquired that gem! Good thing we had it, because we had the new arrivals to take care of. We tiptoed into the house to retrieve a blanket, a pillow for their little heads, and of coarse, a glass doll's bottle. The problem was, where were we going to get some milk for the little critters? We asked politely for a little milk but were told there was none. Mother jokingly said, "Go milk the cow." We took her seriously and went to the pasture to round up the cow. Moochie was a grand old cow, laid-back like an old grandma. We righted her around and tried to figure out who would be best to pull the spigots to get the milk. Us girls won.

The task took us longer than Dad. We tried to remember how he milked, but it was a lot easier said than done. Moochie kinda swatted a fly with her tail and stepped back at the same moment and knocked the pail over, so we had to start at point A again. It took about an hour to get enough milk for the little guys.

We pushed the buggy to the shade of the old maple. There we fed the kittens until they could eat no more. We were overjoyed that we actually milked the cow and had the babies all fed.

When Dad got home from the junkyard, he went out and tried to milk old Moochie, but she didn't have too much to give. Dad couldn't understand why. I think our mother knew, but she didn't say a word.

That night, the kittens disappeared. We were told that their mama came back and got them.

We weren't that disappointed that they were gone, because it was a hard job, milking that darn cow.

———

Neighbors

7

Neighbors

There were very few houses on our road when I was a kid. The Carpenter brothers' was the first place, coming up Hook Road. They farmed and had a small apple orchard. They had large draft horses that did the bulk of the heavy work. They lived in a rambling old farmhouse. In the kitchen, they had a large barrel filled with water. All they had to do was turn the water spigot on in the barrel, and out it came. No electric needed for that; it was all gravity fed from the springs.

Ralph and Carol were bachelors, so they hired a live-in housekeeper to take care of the housework. Her name was Alice. She had brown hair with a small amount of white mixed in. She wore wire-rimmed glasses and was of average build. Alice was very nice, kind-hearted, and would do anything for anyone. She drove a green Chevy coupe, of sorts, very slowly. When I say slowly, I mean slowly. Her top speed might have been fifteen to twenty miles an hour, if that.

Alice attended West Hill Church every Sunday when it was in session. When Bible school was starting, Alice would be the first one to let my mother know. That would mean that we would have to attend. My mother thought it would broaden our horizons, but it didn't. We never attended church, so trying to understand why we had to go to Bible school did not make a lick of sense. Alice would pick us up at a snail's pace and bring us back the same. We dreaded going.

As my sister and I got older, Alice would hire us to help wallpaper. I am not sure how many layers were on the wall, but there was a lot. We would walk early in the morning and arrive there about seven o'clock, about breakfast time for the old gentlemen. I was amazed as I glanced at the table. It was neatly set, and the food was unreal. Large steaks, potatoes, veggies, bread, and other food graced the table. That's what I call a first-class meal. Alice would get righted around and get us to work. We papered many rooms. By the end of the day, we were rather tired. We were paid 25 cents each for our wallpapering. Money is money.

Above the Carpenter farm was the No. 9 school where my dad attended and my aunt Eva Hook taught. Actually, she was my dad's sister-in-law. There was another tiny house that a brook ran under. This was where my parents lived until they moved up to my gram's land, probably due to the rat situations. Apparently, rats lived there, and when my sister was born, they found a rat right next to her crib. That put them in motion, rather quickly, to find better living quarters.

Next was Clarence and Florence Hook's place, my grandparents. That is where we were brought up. Other relatives lived up the road apiece. My aunt and uncle and family of cousins, and then the Felch farm.

We also had a couple of brothers that were from the other side of the hill, Frank and Walter Hayes; they were characters. They would show up barefooted with rolled-up britches, fish poles in hand. Frank laughed a lot and Walt just sucked on his pipe that was tightly clinched between his teeth. Walt worked and Frank stayed home to take care of his mom; she was blind. They also brought up their nephew. They both were hard workers. They had very little money, but they seemed to enjoy life and valued it.

On the East Randolph Road lived the Hoods. I can remember seeing them haying with the draft horses. Some of the large field was rather steep, but the sure-footed animals didn't seem to mind.

One early morning, Mr. Hood got in touch with my dad and said that someone had broken into his house. They had tried to open the old safe. However, they were unable to. In the process, they had ruined the dial on it, and it could not be opened. Later that morning, he arrived at the garage to see if dad could get it opened. He had troubled, sad eyes, worried about something that was in the safe. He said little as he waited. Finally, Dad got it opened, and the old man went forward to see if there was anything missing. The box he was looking for was still there. He wiped his brow with his hand and slowly opened the old box, revealing a long braid of hair. He explained that it was his mother's. He smiled, thanked my dad, and headed back to the farm.

Jack Fitts also lived on the East Randolph Road. He worked for the Barre quarries. Jean, his very understanding wife, gave piano lessons. Jack was a walker. He would walk all over the place, greeting people with his tales and stories.

He would arrive at my parents' place and greet everyone like he had not seen them for years. He would gather up one of my brothers and put him on his knee and start to bounce him up and down while singing, "Trot, trot to Boston to buy a fat pig . . ." over and over again until they wanted to get down, in a very dizzy state.

One day he arrived styling with a new hat. He put it on my brother's head and started to bounce him. Wayne finally was able to escape. He headed directly to the duck pond. He took the hat off his head and placed it in the pond and stirred it around a tad. When Jack was ready to head home, he inquired about his hat. My little brother told him it was in the duck pond. Jack thought he was joking. Finally, he went down to take a look, and sure as rain, there among the duck waste was his newly purchased hat. He retrieved a stick and dug it out and went down the road with the hat dangling in front of him. Arriving home, he asked his wife, Jean, if she would please wash it for him. She asked him if he was bouncing the little boys again. "No wonder they put your hat in the duck pond." The answer to his question was a no. She told him to put it in the brook and let it remain there until it was clean.

Jack would continue to arrive at my parents nearly every week, spinning his yarns and bouncing the boys until they could run faster than him.

———

The Boys in the
Family

The Boys in the Family

The family was given some roller skates. We really didn't have anywhere to use them, because the road and driveway were dirt with a lot of potholes. We knew we could come up with a solution to the problem. Why not have the boys put the roller skates on, and then we can have them hold bailer twine as we ride the bike really fast?

We finally found some bailer twine, but we needed some sort of material to put in the toe of the skates, because they were too big. That problem was solved, and getting on wobbly legs, we took off like lighting, going down the hill as fast as we could, hitting the potholes. The boys were flying high, trying to stay upright. They hit a rock, and they both let go of the twine. A little tattered and a few scrapes, but all was well in the skating world.

Everyone seemed rather bored with just riding down the road. We had to add something more interesting. The idea of lassoing the mean rooster came into mind. Why not? The bird was awful. He would chase you and then do a pecking attack. It was our turn for the skate attack.

The flock was busy plucking bugs, clucking to each other. I imagine they were talking about the weather. They had no idea what was planned. A nod was our signal to go. With our heads down with determination, we were off, heading straight for the flock of birds. In a flash we entered their space, and they went into defense mode. The racket they made was deafening. Feathers were flying, chickens were running. The roosters stuck out their chest.

After the air cleared, we could see what damage was done. The boys did lasso the mean rooster. God knows how they did it. The bird was let loose, and the boys were picked up off the ground. Bruce's glasses were dangling off the side of his head. Other than that, they looked in pretty good shape. At that point, we figured we had better scram, before our mother came out to see what the ruckus was.

Our parents went to spend some time with their friends one afternoon. They left my sister in charge, since she was the oldest. The boys liked to play pranks on her. Wayne, the oldest boy, had thought about it for some time. He disappeared up the stairs. All at once, a mattress came barreling down the stairs. Patty appeared, to see what had happened. She opened the mattress and there Wayne was, with eyes closed and not a twitch.

Patty started crying and carrying on like an uncontrolled nut. She shook him and tried to get him to sit up. When he couldn't take it any longer, he started to roar with laughter. Wrong move. She was about to kill him for that stunt, chasing him around the house, round and around, until they were getting tired. He ran to his room and crawled inside an old bureau that had two small doors and a lock on the inside that he rigged up for this purpose. He stayed in there until our parents came home.

The boys were playing ball in the house. It was forbidden when our parents were home, but they weren't, so the game was on. They tossed the baseball and hit it for a long time, until it went through the two panes of windows.

They were in trouble.

Nope, with the quick wit of Wayne, they were saved. Blame it on the dog. He was chasing an animal, and he accidentally put his paw into the glass and broke it.

The only thing they didn't think about was the hole was almost a perfect circle. Damn, that dog was good.

Usually, on sunny days, you would find the boys under the apple tree playing. They would harness up bugs and have them pull little logs to the pretend sawmill. They did this by using some thread, and very carefully tying it around the bug until it was snug. They would tie the other end to a piece of grass, pretending it was a huge log. They made a little whip that was to resemble an ox whip. It was made from a half-inch piece of straw with a piece of thread on it. They guided the bugs to the log pile at the mill. As the sun started to set, they would lead the bugs to the pasture, where they had spread grass and leaves for their supper and a small tin of water, in case they were thirsty.

Bruce, the youngest, was an animal lover. No matter what he found, dead or alive, he would bring it back to his room. If it passed over to the other side, he would get some tissue, roll it up, and place it in his bureau drawer. The cat was always catching something, a mouse, squirrel, you name it, and there was Bruce charging after the cat and getting the animal out of its mouth before it was bitten too many times. He would try to revive it, and nine times out of ten they were goners. So, there was another one to add to his growing collection. He would neatly place them gently into their last resting place. Or so he thought. After about a week or so the air would reek so badly that Mother would smell it until she found out what it was. There they were all lined up, with their little heads at the top of the drawer, tissue drawn tightly around them, like a blanket, dead as a door nail and stinking to high heaven. She would get a box and take them out, disinfect the area, and bury them under the rose bush. Thank goodness, he finally outgrew this, after about five years.

The oldest, Wayne, loved earthworms. Just ask him. He made money off of them. He would eat one for fifty cents. No kidding, that was really good for your reputation at school. A bug-eating brother—thank goodness, he was younger then me. One day he went out to get his supply of worms. He made the mistake of putting them in his coat pocket for safekeeping. He forgot them for a couple of days, and they had gone all through the lining of his coat. That was the end of his worm eating.

———

The Ad in the
National
Geographic
Magazine

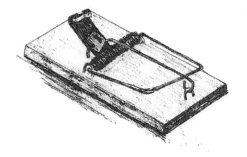

9

The Ad in the National Geographic Magazine

One hot summer day, my brother was looking at an old *National Geographic* magazine. He was lying on the grass under a shade tree, just roaring with laughter. His curly head was bobbing up and down so hard I thought for sure that it would fall off. He just couldn't stop! I went over to see what was so funny. I looked down at the magazine, and I started to laugh. We both nearly peed our pants. Tears were streaming down our faces as we giggled. Finally we stopped to catch our breath. What a find. No it wasn't the people with little on. It was an ad for d-CON.

It was a large colored ad. It took up a quarter of the page. In the ad was a large old man, dressed in a nightcap and shirt. He had snuck down stairs to raid the refrigerator. He had this sandwich all made and was preparing for his first bite, and then it happened. He stepped on a mousetrap, trapping his big hairy toe. He was screaming at the top of his lungs. What was really funny was the little mouse lying on his back, laughing and pounding his fist on the floor. That ad was worth a thousand words or more.

Wayne would take the magazine to the dinner table. Dinner was usually a no-talking time. You know the old saying: Kids were seen but not heard. He would get my attention, and I knew what he wanted, to get a little action going, just to liven things up. Nudging me—I could not contain my laughter. That would be it. We would both start laughing so hard that we were told to leave the table. Dad would be madder than a wet hen. He would take the magazine and throw it away, but we always had a supply of them. We had stacks of them, tied up with bailer twine, ready for the right moment.

————

The Junkyard

10

The Junkyard

My father had a junkyard for used parts. Abandoned vehicles of all shapes and sizes lined up like a used-car lot. Us kids would use it like a playground, playing hide-and-seek, pretending we were cops and robbers, Bonnie and Clyde. Our imagination would run wild. Sometimes we would spend all day there. I can still remember the smell of the steering wheel. It was a good smell, but it was hard to describe. The interiors of these big toys were rather clean, with no clutter. Usually, all four of us would pile in and take turns driving.

One sunny morning, my brother disappeared with the dog. No matter how much we searched and called, he did not answer. It was two or three hours before we finally found him, out like a light, sleeping on top of old Tootie in the junk car. My mother wasn't too concerned because the dog was with him. She knew that he would be safe.

One beautiful June day, my brother and I went out to the junkyard and climbed up on top of the hood of an old rusty school bus. Using the windshield as a backrest, we reclined and started to eat the green apples that were dangling from the tree above our heads. We were told not to eat them because we would get sick, but we ate them anyways. We were trying to come up with something to do that was fun and adventurous. Finally, we came up with a plan.

Sliding off the hood to the ground, off we went to see if we could find anything of value stashed in any of the cars. We usually found something we thought was worth something, but this time we got more then we bargained for. We got into the nettles.

Our legs and arms started to sting like crazy. We were warned not to get into them, so we knew better than to go back and ask Mother for some ointment. We figured we might as well climb back up on the school bus and eat more apples. We bit the little apples in half and lined them up on our legs to get a good supply in case our arms got tired from picking them. To our amazement there was no more stinging. It must be the apples!

We started rubbing the bitten apples all over our arms and legs. A miracle of miracles! We found a cure for nettles. Leaning back against the windshield, we ate the forbidden little green apples and laughed about getting in the nettles and finding something that would make the stinging go away. Little green apples, good for the soul and nettles. If Mother only knew.

We spent many hours in the junkyard, and Dad finally gave in to the crushers. They arrived, and no more junkyard.

———

Skyward and
Other Things

11

Skyward and Other Things

The roar of the plane would send us scrambling for the open pasture to see if the plane was going to drop some shiny treasure that we would retrieve and put in a little box for safekeeping.

The treasure was like aluminum foil, shredded into strips, about a half-inch wide and in various lengths. We would run around like the mad hatter and collect as much as we could, before someone else found it. We asked why these strips were being dropped, and as I recall the answer was to scramble the airwaves so that the enemies of our country wouldn't know what the government was doing. This went on for many summers of our youth.

Another great sight was the enormous war planes that would be fueled in the air by another plane. We would lie on our backs and watch with amazement at the sight, wondering how they could fuel up and not run into each other. We all had our theories, but it came down to being a superpilot.

Weather balloons were another wonder. We

would chase after the orange red ball and hope it would land, so we could get a closer look at it.

At last, one of the weather balloons was spotted dangling from a branch of the old maple. We could hardly contain our excitement. Dad finally climbed the tree and retrieved the battered balloon and little container.

Our father had a wealth of information on almost everything. He was always reading about different things, such as windmills, water wheels —actually, anything regarding science experiments. We surrounded him, waiting for him to begin, and we were not disappointed.

Dad explained to us that the weather balloon collected valuable data about the atmospheric weather conditions. The information is used for weather prediction and tracking the weather. The instruments in the balloon are called a radiosonde. This is suspended from the balloon by a cord or rope. When the weather balloon reached a certain altitude, it would explode and float back to earth, to be found by a tracking device.

We also asked what the balloon was made of. Dad replied that it was made out of flexible material, such as latex. He further explained that it was inflated with helium or hydrogen so it could fly.

Dad sent the balloon back, as instructed.

The T-Shirt

12

The T-Shirt

In our early childhood, our mother would send us out to play. It was early in the morning, right after Dad left for work. It would be really cold, sometimes unbearable. We would head for our playhouse, which was an old car without the wheels. Inside the old car, the walls were velvet. There were velvet shades on the old windows that actually worked. The floorboard was wood and still in good condition. We would sit on the broken rocking chair with a red leather seat and brass tacks. It was lovely in its day. There we would sit and wait for the sun to bring warmth back into our beings. Soon it would get too hot inside. We would venture out and find something to do.

We played cowboys and rode the cows as our favorite steeds. We were told not to put our cowgirl outfits on, but kids being kids, we thought, Why not? I wanted to be Annie Oakley, my hero of heroes. Actually, I wanted to grow up just like her.

My sister and I stripped down and placed our clothes carefully on the barbed-wire fence in a place that the big people wouldn't notice, and off we went. We played all day, and finally it was time to help with supper. We wandered over to the fence where our clothes were stashed, but half of them were gone, vanished into thin air.

Old Moochie was standing there, chewing her cud, like she didn't have a care in the world. She wanted her ears scratched, and we obliged. All at once our eyes almost popped out of our heads. Moochie wasn't just chewing grass, it appeared, for there were stripes in her mouth.

Have you ever tried to get something out of a cow's mouth? It ain't easy. We tried to get her to drop it, like our old dog, but that failed. She just eyed us and continued to chew.

We had to do something fast, for Mother would skin us alive. Better yet, she would wring our necks.

We finally came up with a plan. My sister was to pry the mouth open, and I was the lucky one to stick my hands in and pull the shirts out. Easier said than done. The problem was, she kept on swallowing them, so we had to wait through the cycle. God knows how many cycles went through.

Finally, a window of opportunity. It was now or never. I didn't dare to blink, fearing I would miss once again. I grabbed the edge and pulled with all my might, landing in a heap at Moochie's feet. Finally, victory. We hooted and hollered, and then drat, the shirts were the color of grass, and they had teeth holes on every inch of material. We were totally dead.

There must be a way to get out of this predicament. Sure enough: Light bulb. Brainstorm. We circled around the trailer to make sure no one was outside to spoil our plan.

We creeped up to the clothesline and pulled

two clean T-shirts off. We pulled the shirts quickly over our heads. There, in turn, we hung the holey green grass-stained shirts on the line with the clean clothes. To make it really believable, we let the cows out. They milled around the clothesline, batting the clothing with their tail, chewing on some. Sure as rain, they were going to believe it.

My parents never mentioned anything about the holey shirts or the cows being out. We did sweat bullets for a couple of days, and then we figured we were home free.

I was sure glad that we were such good problem solvers.

———

The Road Crew

13

The Road Crew

When I was growing up, in the fifties and sixties, the roads were mostly raked by hand. The men would start early in the morning, before it got too hot, and start tending to the road, raking and doing whatever else had to be done.

My grandfather was one of the workers. He usually was dressed in bib overalls, a T-shirt, and some sort of head covering. Actually, all the men seemed to have the same style of dressing. He was very short and thin, with whiskers on his lined face. He reminded me of Willie Nelson. He smoked Camels and chewed Red Man tobacco. Just like all the rest of the crew.

When the crew was working on our dirt road, we really enjoyed them. They seemed to plan it that they would be in front of my parents about lunchtime. My parents let us join them for lunch. They usually had something extra for us, such as an apple, orange, cookies, or a sugar cube. Grandfather would have sugar cubes, because he was a diabetic.

We would sit on the side of the road and think we were one of the crew. They would treat us that way. They would carry on a conversation about anything.

After lunch was over, they would continue up the road. We watched them until they were out of sight. With one last wave, we would return to our chores or playing.

———

Ms. Hattie and
Mr. Charles

14

Ms. Hattie and Mr. Charles

The arrival of Mr. and Mrs. Adams broke the boredom of the weekend. They were a very lively couple, a cute couple. They would hold hands, he would hold the door for her, help her with her coat on and off, and pull her chair out for her. They were dressed in Saturday-go-to-meeting attire. He was usually in a suit with a fedora hat, which he removed when he entered. She was in a fashionable dress with a fancy hat.

We were taught from a young age you were to be seen and not heard. Not a good thing if you liked to talk.

We said our hellos and gave each a hug and went about our business. At that point, I didn't know what my business might be that day. I wandered up the stairwell, eyeballing the tin cans of buttons and marbles my mother collected. Of course, the tops were missing.

Entering the bedroom, I tried hard to think of something useful to do.

At the age of seven or eight, you had to have an imagination, however big or small, to entertain oneself. I decided to dress up in one of Gram's old outfits of yesteryear, long and flowing, and a hat with plumage and flowers and a big brim. To top it off, my gram's fancy satin gloves that were to go up to your elbows, but they went up to nearly my armpits. I righted the buttons so they were straight.

Looking in the mirror, I knew there was something missing, but what? I looked from the top of my head to the top of my toes. Oh, right, a pair of dancing shoes. Mother had a closet in the hallway. There they were, gleaming satin, off-white. Oh, my, what a sight. Stilettos!

I put those puppies on and paraded around the room. I looked into the old closet in the bedroom and found an old lantern that was dusty, but it would work. I was going to be a ghost, an interesting one at that.

I started swinging the lantern and in a loud whisper, started to chant, "Yoo-hoo, lantern," over and over.

I heard the company ask, "What in the world is that?" My parents didn't really have an answer. They didn't even want to know what I was up to.

I had a brainstorm at that very minute. I could waltz through the kitchen with my outfit on. They said "seen but not heard."

I crept to the edge of the stairs. The mighty stilettos were giving me a hard time. I figured if Mother could walk in them, anyone should be able to. Yeah, right, I thought.

I started down the stairs. I set the lantern down. I figured I didn't really need it for just a walk-through.

I had no sooner got my foot on the second step than I knew I was in trouble. The next thing I knew, I was flying through the air. I landed spread-eagled at the bottom of the stairs.

I thought I was in a war zone. The marbles

were bouncing down the stairs like rockets. It finally died down to a dull roar. I lay there for a moment. I wiggled my fingers and toes, my legs, and finally my arms. Nothing broken, at least.

I couldn't see anything. Drat, I am blind. No, I said to myself, just open your eyes. I did that. Darkness. I reached up and touched my head. Oh, yeah, the hat. Lift the hat.

I lifted the brim, slowly, to see what expression was on their faces. I figured I could save some of my dignity. I scraped myself off of the floor, adjusting my hat, fixing the plumage, trying to get the wrinkles out of the outfit, and then adjusting my gloves. My mother was rather upset, could tell by her look. But the company started to laugh with glee. You made our day, they said.

I looked up at the ceiling and whispered to Gram, This was a good one. I made people laugh, got a rise out of my mother, and I didn't break the darn stiletto heel off.

———

My
Five-Dollar Bike

My Five-Dollar Bike

B ack when I was a kid, during the 1950s and 1960s, money was tight. You only needed certain things in order to live, and a bicycle wasn't one of them. You could look all you wanted, at all the fancy ones in the Sears and Roebuck catalog, but that was the end of it. All the village kids and some of the lucky hill kids would jump on their wonder machine and set sail down the hill, with hoots and whistles, and reappear at the next ridge. I would look at them and pretend it was I who was sailing down the hill.

My father worked at my step-grandfather's junkyard in Randolph Center. He would bring home the damndest things, from old cast-iron kettles to a doctor's surgery table.

But one day was a day of wonders. Out of his old beat-up Pontiac station wagon, with the face of Pontiac still intact on the hood, a bicycle appeared. Like magic, there it was. Everyone wanted to be the first, so the youngest went first and then it was my turn. I pushed that puppy clear to the top of the hill, popped on like it was a steed, and went just as fast as I could down the hill. I prayed that it would stop before I landed in the frog pond. The reason for that was the bicycle had no brakes. For that matter, it had no chain and no tires, just the rims. But the wheels went around; that was all that mattered. We all took turns on it and never grew tired of it. We did, however, paint it forest green. What a sight to behold.

I still longed for my own bike. One of my friends at school told me one day that she was getting a new bike and she was selling her old one for five dollars. I wanted that bike so bad. I had to think about making some fast dough. I had been babysitting with my sister nearly every Friday and Saturday night for Shod and Sally. They had four kids, and they liked to go honky-tonking. At one point, they lived down the road at the old Loughy homestead, so it wasn't too far to go.

I figured it would take at least a month, perhaps more, to save enough to get my dream machine.

The day finally arrived. Dad took me down to the village, and then we went up Court Street to the Archer home. Sally was there with her brand-new bike, with the brake lever on the handlebars, waiting for my arrival. I carefully counted out the ones and quarters and handed it to her. She went to the garage and came out with my pride and joy, a gleaming powder-blue bike. Dad opened the station wagon door and put it in the back and headed home.

I really had a blast with that bike. It wasn't as sleek as the new ones, but it was solid, and it fit the bill.

I had many adventures on that mighty machine.

Up the road from where we lived a family from Bridgeport, Connecticut, had purchased the old Felch farm. It was in the middle of nowhere, and I mean nowhere. A truck hardly dared to go down that road, much less a car. The house was in disrepair, windows broken, doors hanging by a thread, grass growing through the screen door. You didn't dare to go in, due to the critters that might have moved in. The family would come up and stay for a few weeks a year—a very talented family. He was a doctor, she was a nurse. The six kids were into playing cellos and any other instrument you could think of, talented little buggers. I really enjoyed their company. They asked if we would keep an eye on their rustic living headquarters. We told them we would. Sometimes only one of us would venture up.

It was a rather beautiful day. I was enjoying every second of the ride. I was listening to all the sounds, taking in the spring air and feeling the gentle breeze on my face. Arriving at the old farm, I checked the doors and windows to make sure they were still locked. The farmstead looked fine, so I headed back down the hill.

I was halfway home when a deer nearly knocked me off the bike. I slammed on the brakes as hard as I could and stopped. The deer hit my front tire. I looked to my right, because there was movement, and there was the biggest black panther that I had ever seen! It looked just like a mountain lion, but it was sleek black. I thought, "Oh, Lord, I've had the radish this time." The cat was inches from me, bearing down. He took a slight detour to avoid the bike, messing up his concentration on his meal. The giant cat leaped through the air and landed on the bank, and he vanished. The bike held its own. I nearly landed flat on my face, but for some reason I held my balance. It happened so fast that I didn't have time to be scared. I caught my breath and listened to the woods' noises, and suddenly it grew silent. Total silence. I gathered my senses, and I rode like a lightning bolt down the hill, not stopping until I was safe at home.

The black panthers were seen often. No one knows where they came from. One thought was perhaps someone had them for pets and they discovered that they weren't pet material and they let them free. The last one I saw was in West Braintree right after the first snow a few years ago.

———

The Music Man

16

The Music Man

M usic was a big part of our lives back when television was not viewed 24/7. My grandmother Hook had a piano that was bought brand-new back in the 1920s by my grandpa. It was treated with great respect; not just anybody would be allowed to play it. Gram would let my sister and me play it, but not my brothers.

My Grandfather LaFrancis could play just about anything. He would be dressed in his usual attire, bib overalls, a cigarette dangling from his lips and his hair going every which way. He looked a lot like Willie Nelson. He would grab the fiddle and start playing, and my grandmother would jump up to the piano and start pounding the keys like her life depended on it. She looked like Jo Ann Castle, famed piano player from *The Lawrence Welk Show*, with her head swaying back and forth at a high rate of speed; you would think it would detach and go into orbit. Her feet were keeping time at a mad rate, and her hands would fly across the ivories, making the music into magic. The objects on the piano would jump up and down with every beat; usually a photo would drop off the edge.

Not only could Grandpa play the fiddle, he was an ace on the banjo, beetle-back mandolin, guitar, and last but not least, the harmonica. By late in the evening, he would grab the harmonica and start wailing on it. By then, he'd had a few pops and was feeling no pain, but could he play. You name the song, and he was on it. He would sit cross-legged, and he would finally topple over into a little heap. One of my uncles would pick him up and he would be still playing, without missing a beat.

If only the younger generation would turn off all of their gadgets for an hour or so and just listen to the magic of the old-time music.

———

Stairway to Heaven

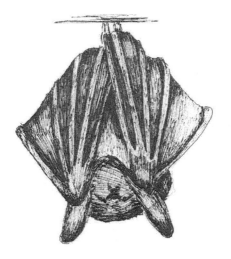

17

Stairway to Heaven

We moved into my grandparents' house a few years after my gram passed. It was a whole different world. We had space—space for a kitchen table so we could all sit down and eat. We only had a tiny table that Mother made her bread on to sell. We had a bathroom in the house, but it was never used. Don't ask; I don't have the answer to that. We still used the outdoor privy, for a number of years. We took teacup baths; it seemed forever before the plumbing was finished. It sometimes appeared that my father did not like change. The downstairs also had two other rooms. My brothers had their own rooms. Upstairs were two bedrooms, my parents' and us girls' bedrooms. But I found the most amazing rooms were in the back shed. I believe you call it a Dutch oven. It was a room surrounded by handmade bricks from down the road. It had three or four ovens in it. It was really amazing. I was saddened when my father tore it apart.

The back shed consisted of a tiny room and two rooms with fireplaces. In the summer, I loved to sleep there. My own space, to think and dream.

The attic was another place that was fun to explore. It had its own private stairway. After my chores were completed, I would head up the dark stairwell to see what treasures I could find. Finding treasures was really fun. I found all sorts of things in the cracks of the floor. I found a gold locket that was of my grandparents. Old coins were found a lot.

I really wanted to call it my bedroom. My parents agreed that I could stay in there during the spring and fall. They probably figured it would help the disagreements my sister and I had, most likely daily.

I moved in my bed, table, chair, my small amount of clothing, and I was in my own little world.

I had one window that overlooked the old shack we had lived in. It was a reminder where we came from. I read, wrote short poems, played guitar, and daydreamed.

I was in the attic for a few days. I kept feeling something go past my face nearly every night. I wasn't scared; I just wanted to learn what it was. A few days later, I finally found out what it was: a very small bat.

Of course, I named him Batty.

I was in his space, and he let me know it. I guess we finally came to an agreement. He would hang from the rafters and kind of swing in the breeze. He was really funny to watch. He was my little companion, until I left to be on my own.

———

The Quilt of Many Colors

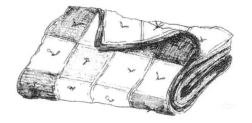

18

The Quilt of Many Colors

M y mother was a very good artist and craftswoman. She would take someone's cast-off item and make it into a piece of art. One thing that stood out were her quilts, which she made from our outgrown clothing and other people's outdated items that were decades old or more. They were of many prints and colors, and they were made of cotton, wool, silk, leather, and other material. I can still look at the squares and remember what article of clothing they came from.

When we were in school, there was a dress code, which was enforced by the principal and the school board—to say nothing about our parents; they were really strict. If the garment was not correct, we had to change before the bus arrived. We most always wore items that were given to us, hand-me-downs from who-knows-where. You had to wear what you had.

When we were young, it didn't matter, because we really weren't into fashion. We were more interested in learning than worrying about the style and color combinations we wore. When we hit graded school, it was pretty bad. You were taunted and called names. The only escape was a tree and a book. Climbing as high as you could and sitting there on a limb, hearing or seeing nothing below, shutting off the world itself. I was told you could go anywhere in the world and beyond by putting yourself into a book. I know it was true, because that is how I survived going through school.

When we entered high school, short dresses were the latest rage. Nearly everyone wore a miniskirt or dress, but a few had to go by their parent's strict rules, and we were one of them. Nothing shorter than in the middle of your knee or longer. The dress code had been lifted by then. You were able to wear whatever you wanted. That meant jeans and pants. I thought that was great, but the parents said no way. They didn't care if it was hot or forty below, we still had to wear dresses. Perhaps that's why I don't wear too many of them today.

So you see why I probably remember each little square. They represented my life for twelve years.

I still have the quilts my mother made. One is really large, and it is double-sided and hand-tied. It is used on the coldest of nights and given a rest in the warm weather. Some of the labels of the clothing companies were put in the squares to remind me that, at some point, this piece of clothing was very fashionable and probably expensive, decades ago.

————

The Cast Iron

19

The Cast Iron

A lot of people think I am touched in the head, even some of my friends. I don't think touched is the right word, but perhaps close. You see, I love cast iron. Pots, stoves, you name it, if it is cast iron, I want it. The ceiling rafters are held down by my beloved cast-iron pots. My gram's legged kettle, fry pans of any size and shape, muffin pans, gem pans, chicken fryers, griddles, waffle makers—I tell you, they are one of the most beautiful objects that man made.

When a new person comes to the cabin, his or her eyes dart from the deer-head covered walls to the ceiling with all the gleaming black treasures. Some people don't dare to ask; they just think, Who in their right mind wants all that old stuff on the ceiling? The people who show some interest will get the short or long version of "The Cast-Iron Story," depending on their attention span. You can tell that by how long they stare at it with wonder in their eyes.

It all started a long time ago. Everyone used cast iron. If you didn't have a couple of pieces, you probably didn't cook. My parents and grandparents all had numerous pieces. We were blessed, because Dad worked at the junkyard, and he would bring home some jim-dandies. Word spread about my cast iron, far and wide. Friends would show up with a sad piece of cast iron to see if I wanted it. Darn tooting, I would love to take it off their hands. It may look like it was on its last legs, ready to go to cast-iron heaven, but with a little bit of elbow grease, it can be revived to its natural beauty. It may take weeks, sometimes longer, to get just the right slide on the bottom of the gentle giant. You pry the rust and other material that has layered up for years, with a knife, a screwdriver, or whatever works. Finally, you are at the stage where it looks wonderful. You apply mineral oil, and put it in the oven, and slowly let the oil do its work. What a thing of beauty.

Way back when, they weren't washed much. I am surprised we didn't die of food poisoning. After frying bacon, the grease was left in it, for weeks, used and reused. When it was cleaned, it was a bit of salt and taking a cloth and wiping it out. Hot water and soap was never used. They would say it would ruin the pan.

This is where I am a little bit different. After I left home, I thought about the germs and decided to start using hot water and soap. I dry it by putting it on top of a warm stove or in the warm oven, leaving it there until completely dry. Then I wipe it with an oil-covered cloth. For years I used vegetable oil, but an old man who loved cast iron as much as I do told me to use mineral oil. It is used by humans, and it doesn't leave an after-taste, and it doesn't go rancid. He was so right.

I counted the beautiful beauties: I have over seventy-five pieces hanging from the rafters. I tell some people that in case of a hurricane, it will keep the roof from flying off. The collection is still growing. We also have an eighteen-inch kettle. It hardly fits in the oven. You can cook a twenty-pound turkey in it. The bonus was, it came with a cover. It's real old, and it was thirty-five bucks. What a deal.

We go to Maine in August. We found a piece that we had to have. It was a griddle, approximately twenty by thirty inches, and it came from an old logging camp. We bought it, but where on the Harley do you put it? It weighed close to twenty pounds. The answer: Call your friends that live there, and when they visit you, they will bring it with them.

We have the best of both worlds.

Honestly, if I am feeling poorly, just send me to a flea market, yard sale, or antique shop. I will be cured in a matter of seconds when I eyeball the perfect piece.

A great friend of mine, Sid Godfrey, gave me a lovely old kettle, one of a kind. I named it the Sid Pot. The pot is to die for. It has a clover on it and a vent hole at the top. I use it a lot. As Sid handed me my birthday pot, he said that he knew I was a tad touched about cast iron, and I was far from normal. The question is, what is normal? I did look it up, decided why do I want to be normal? There is no adventure or fun in that.

———

The Planting and Harvesting of Our Food

The Planting and Harvesting of Our Food

This time of year, the smell of spring is in the air. Everywhere you look is a rebirth of sorts. The sounds of the birds' songs fill the still air with a magic for living.

This brings back a lot of memories, of the 1950s and 1960s. When we were probably about six or seven, my sister and I would take a bushel basket and head for the fields to dig dandelion greens. When the basket was filled, we headed back to the water house and cleaned them. It took some patience to get all the dried grass and field soil off of them. We would help Mother put the greens in a glass canning jar and put it through the pressure cooker. It seemed like hours that we waited, with dangling legs, over the old high chair. The pressure cookers were different than the ones we have today. There was a gauge on them, and you had to get the greens to a certain pressure and then lower the heat—but make sure it maintained the pressure—for a given amount of time. I remember sitting there for hours, watching the gauge and just wanting to be outside.

My grandmother used to tell a story about my

uncle, regarding canning. He was watching the same canner but probably daydreaming, and he forgot what he was doing. The canner blew up and put a hole in the ceiling. My eyes would dart to the ceiling, where the outline of the canner lid was still visible, a reminder to watch the gauge, because the same thing could happen to you. What a dreadful thought.

After the greens were canned, they were toted down to the cellar, where they remained until needed.

The garden planting started after dandelion season. The potatoes would go in, probably two hundred pounds of them. If we had the money, Dad would get seed potatoes from the grain store; if not, he would save some of the ones that we harvested from the year before and plant them.

All of us were involved with the planting. Dad had a doodlebug (he never owned a tractor), and he would plow and harrow the potato pieces and then take an old horse plow he rigged up to make the rows.

The next planting was the regular garden. The usual corn, string beans, kidney beans, shell beans, all sorts of squashes, tomatoes, onions, et cetera, were planted in the huge gardens. There were usually three or four areas that we would plant. Every year the gardens were rotated. If you didn't do this, the gardens would be full of disease and unwanted insects, say nothing about depleting the soil.

When the first little green shoots would appear through the warm earth, the weeding would start. That was a chore and a half. At the time, it seemed that was all we did. It wasn't, of course.

The haying came next. My sister and I were taught how to run the doodlebug. We were so small that we had to stand in order to see over the steering wheel. At a snail's pace, we would be off. My father would cut the hay. Mother would rack it and throw the loose hay on the wagon. It also had to be tramped down so we could get a lot more hay on the wagon. With the wagon over-flowing with the sweet dry hay, we would go to the hay mow, where we would unload the precious winter food for the cows.

In August, we would start to harvest and can our vegetables. From early morning until the dusk arrived, we canned. We usually put away between eight hundred and one thousand quarts of our winter food supply. You would can all you had, because the next year might not yield anything, due to the weather, bugs, or blight.

The root vegetables, consisting of onions, carrots, turnips, beets, potatoes, squash, pumpkins, et cetera, all went into the cool cellar.

We also raised our own meat. We raised hogs, beef, chickens, and ducks. Mr. Felch would make his rounds to the area farms to kill the animals and prepare them. Dad made the hog up into a lot of hams. He had an old barrel where he built a fire a certain way to smoke the hams. He also made salt pork and bacon. Every part of the animal was used. Nothing was wasted.

The beef was mostly canned. When my grandmother bought a freezer, we would freeze some. (It seemed rather funny that we had a freezer but no refrigerator.)

The chickens and ducks provided us with eggs and meat.

Fall was for coon hunting. All of us kids would pile into our old out-of-date car, along with our old redbone dog. Dad would be in the driver's seat. Off we would go. Dad and the grown-ups would let the dog out, and he would find a coon and tree it, and the grown-ups would shoot it. We stayed in the dark ghostly car, waiting for the return of the hunters. A lot of times, it was scary, but since we were the oldest, you couldn't tell the younger ones that you might be a tad scared.

One night, we were staring out into the night when someone came to the car and started knocking on the window. We had no idea who it was at the time, for we were miles from anyone or any place. We rolled the window down a bit, letting the stale hot air out. The short fat little man had a funny hat on and a uniform on. Dang, if he didn't have a badge on!

We were taught not to talk to strangers, much less roll down the window.

His badge gleamed in the light of his flash-light. He also had a gun at his side, say nothing about the other person that was with him. He asked what our names were.

Do we dare to tell him or not? Where is Dad when you need him?

My brother spoke up and said, "My dad's out catching coons. He's coon hunting."

The badge man said, "I don't think so. He's out shooting deer, isn't he?"

We all replied at once, "No. Dad and our dog are out catching coons."

This conversation went on for a while. There was no way that we were going to convince them that our dad wasn't shooting deer. Finally, shots were fired, yelps, barks, and whining from the dog were coming from over by the tree line. The badge man ran as fast as his little legs could carry him to arrest whoever it was deer jacking, but he had wasted his time tonight, because he was after the wrong man. The one that reported our dad was the true jacker.

We did get a number of coon that night for the freezer.

Coon was a big part of our meals back then. They weren't as sickly as they are now. Mom would cook them in vinegar to tenderize them. They had a lot of fat on them, and Mother made sure that the fat was all taken off.

We also ate woodchuck, rabbits, and other wild game.

Deer hunting was in November. Nearly every family in the hills would get their license and head to their favorite hunting area. Sometimes the family would get a deer. After they harvested it, they hung it upside down for a while, to tenderize it. Then it was cut up and usually canned.

We learned how to survive on very little. I am glad that I was brought up in that time. We learned how to make do with what you had.

There were only a few years in my life that I haven't raised a garden. In 2010, we canned or froze over four hundred quarts of vegetables. Four hundred pounds of potatoes, a bushel of onions, many different types of squash, pumpkins, et cetera, were put in cool storage.

Doug harvested a deer and an elk. The meat was canned and froze. Fish were caught and were put in the freezer. We purchased forty pounds of fresh chicken and that was put away. We only go to the grocery store for very little. I really love to go down to the storage room and open the doors to the cupboards to look at all the beautiful colored canned goods, knowing that if we were unable to go out for months, we still have everything we need and can survive.

———

About the Author

Shirly Hook grew up on West Hill in Chelsea, Vermont, where most of the stories in *My Bring Up* took place. She has never lost her sense of adventure or her sense of humor. She and her family still live in her beautiful state of Vermont. Shirly is a citizen of the Koasek Traditional Band of the Koas Abenaki Nation, and she serves on the Council of Chiefs.

About the Illustrator

Amy Hook-Therrien is the youngest daughter of author Shirly Hook. She received a BFA from the University of Maine in Orono with a focus on painting and sculpture. She lives in Windsor, Vermont, with her husband, Alex.

facebook.com/amy.hook.therrien.art

instagram.com/hooktherrienart